Japan

After the Tsunami

Stephen Platt

www.leveretpublishing.com

Japan 2013
First published - December 2016
Second Edition - September 2017
Published by
Leveret Publishing
56 Covent Garden, Cambridge, CB1 2HR, UK

ISBN 978-1-9124600-4-5

Japan
after the earthquake

Japan 2013

Tohoku - Sendai region

The EEFIT mission visited most of the places affected by the Great Eastern Japan Earthquake 2011 from Sendai north to Kamaishi and south to Fukushima.

Tohoku

Thursday 30 May
From the windows of the airport in Hong Kong there is a view of velvet green mountains and silver skyscrapers and from the silver Narita express women in green paddy fields with water up to their shins.

The short walk from Sendai Station to the Comfort Hotel looks like a set from Blade Runner. We went out to eat sushi and tempura with Tony and David from the UK and Maki, Farnaz and Ryo from Kyoto University.

Friday 1 June, Yuriage, Natori

I slept well and was woken at five by a parliament of rooks. In the lobby the receptionist gave me the SIM card I had ordered over the Internet to be able to use my phone to find where I am when I'm out on my own.

At eleven we met Prof Masato Motosaki, a rather droopy man with Buddy Holly glasses who said the issue was how to recover as quickly as possible. Our bus takes us to Arahama village and we visit a Shinto shrine and then drive down to the coast. The whole area has been cleared, leaving only concrete stumps of houses. This must have been a prosperous and pleasant area to live. A woman has a stall at the roadside with a petition asking the government to allow people to rebuild on their own plots, but the plan is to move people back at least a kilometre behind a new 6m barrier.

One old man has returned to a shack he's built from reclaimed material and blue plastic sheeting. He looks spare and tough in his black motorbike gear, with a white scarf tied around his forehead like a kamikaze pilot. He was being interviewed by a local TV company. We went and talked to one of the workers in the incinerator plant where they sort the debris and burn what they cannot recycle.

We continue to Yuriage, a fishing port at the mouth of the Natori-Gawa River. There are a few remaining

'Kamikazi' protestor, Arahama

Yuriage school clock stopped at 2:45

houses and the odd shrine dotted about the plain, but most have been washed away. There are plans to reduce the built-up area by half. The spit that defended the river mouth and harbour has been scarred away but they are already rebuilding the seawall defences.

We visited two schools. At the first the clock stopped at 2.46 when the earthquake struck and the power failed. At the second school we enter the hall were lost personal possessions have been sorted and laid out. The mud has been washed off but they're still dirt encrusted. Dresses and handbags have been hung on the gym bars. There are piles of school satchels, shoes, cameras, musical instruments, pots and pans, household shrines, records, and, most poignant of all, scrapbooks and family albums of photographs. I leaf through them wondering about their lost lives.

We climb an ancient hill that had housed a shrine where people ran to shelter but had been overwhelmed by the tsunami. It was very sobering standing there, high up, looking out to sea and imagining the terror. Tony talked

Lost photographs

School satchels piled in Yuriage school hall

about how they care for the dead in Japan and try to identify the bodies. Only 300 out of 15-16,000 they had found remained unidentified. But over 2,600 people are still missing.

Here in Sendai, where the land is flat, the wave was 4m high, but further north, on the Rias coast, where there are fiord-like like inlets, the wave was much greater. We went to Iwanuma city, near the airport, where they are creating artificial 10m high hills as a commemorative park. Together with the long sea wall, it looks expensive and elaborate. As we drive back we pass new houses being built 5-6 km inland. This is where the survivors who could afford not to wait for a government house have moved.

We go for dinner in a restaurant opposite the hotel. It didn't look great from outside but turns out to be good. The table is a long low bench with a sunken area for one's legs. We meet Roger Olshansky, an American academic from Illinois on sabbatical leave in Kyoto.

New 5m. embankment Sendai

Saturday 2 June, Utatsu and Shizugawa, Onagawa

We drive further up the coast to Utatsu and Shizugawa. On the coach I sit next to David Alexander from UCL. It is hillier here and buildings that were presumed to be safe, like the disaster management centre at Minamisnariku,

Disaster management centre, Minamisanriku

were over-topped. This is the place where the woman stayed at her post broadcasting a warning until the wave swept through the building. At a temporary container-village I find a fast-food stall and order a fish fritter, with an ice cream to follow, and sit on a plastic garden chair in the sunshine to eat.

We drive to Ishinomaki where a quarter of the buildings were destroyed. The large paper mill is back in production after 15 months, its closure having caused a paper shortage. There are new temporary warehouses in white canvas on tubular frames but the fishing port is still working at less than half capacity.

In the next port across the peninsula, Onagawa, the wave, funnelled by a narrow bay, rose to 18 metres, overwhelming the raised hospital mound and flooding the ground floor to a depth of 2 metres. Anawat describes how the bank manager in the branch in the harbour insisted that the staff stay in the building for security and all had perished. They will raise the port area by a meter and raise the road to act as a barrier.

Emily and I walk over to examine buildings of 3-4 stories that, unable to resist the force of the water, had been overturned and left lying on their sides, ugly and obscene. The concrete piles that had anchored them to the ground

Overturned building, Onagawa

had been ripped out and fractured, leaving the buildings as vulnerable as beached whales.

We have interviews tomorrow with the municipal authorities in Ishinomaki and when we get back to the hotel I venture forth to find brush and polish to heal my battered shoes. I find a department store near the station and what I need and get back to the hotel in time to brush off the day's dust and get down to the lobby to meet the others. We go to the same place as last night and I get chatting to Carlos about Venezuela.

Sunday 3 June, Ishinomaki

Today we are interviewing people in a development company and planners in Ishinomaki. I wake early, soon after five, and shower and read for a while before trying to clarify the questions I'd worked late last night. We are told how the developers worked with stakeholders and local authority people to identify projects to help revitalise the place. Two projects are already committed and after the meeting we go to look at them. They are both on small plots that families have decided to develop into shops and housing. About half the homes will be for displaced people and managed by the municipality. One of the plots is around a beautiful old house that may become an art gallery.

We have lunch in the department store in which the municipal offices are temporarily housed on the upper floors. The standard Japanese 'aeroplane' style meal is called a Bento – I choose salmon. The people we have come to see are in a special reconstruction department of 137 staff that is beginning

Developers, Ishinomaki

Future art gallery, Ishinomaki

to implement the plans to move everyone who lived near the coast to four or five new areas that used to be paddy fields. They needed Government permission for the change of use from agriculture to housing.

The planners said that they consulted residents, but only after everything was decided. There is a problem; along the coast where 40 small fishing villages were destroyed, the people aren't happy. The government wants to move the houses to higher ground by carving new terraces out of the mountain. The people used to have large gardens and allotments and grew their own food and are largely self-sufficient. In the new places they will have only a third of the size of plot. But that's not all; only some of the village ports will be raised and repaired with new harbour walls. It is not clear how they will decide which.

We go to see a camp on the north-west side of the city near the University. The containers are the best we've seen. Some have colourful murals of flowers or fish on the outside walls. The cabins have two small rooms about 2 ½ x 3 m and a kitchenette and bathroom. People have created DIY porches for the snow and to store their household stuff. We speak to residents. One man says he and his wife left it too late and had been caught by the wave and nearly lost their lives. He doesn't want to go back to the same area. We speak to a woman who worked at the museum and had gone home and been caught before she could get to higher ground. The water had come up to the second floor and she had spent a day on a top bunk bed until rescued. Both couples are low priority and may have to wait another couple of years.

On leaving we stop to look at the courtyard farmhouse at the base of the hill. They are beautiful ancient timber structures with gatehouses. We speak

Temporary housing, Ishinomaki

to one of the owners who says her family have lived here for 19 generations. The main house used to be thatched but had recently been modernised with shiny tiles. Two new houses are being constructed on a plot directly in front so perhaps they sold the land. There seems to be a lot of new building further up the road. Two women are tending their vegetable plot – a beautifully mounded soil ridge with neat rows of vegetables.

On the way back we drive along the coast passed the famous Matushima Islands. The hotels were protected by the line of islands that acted like a reef that broke the power of the wave. But the wave hit the peninsula south of the resort and many people who had sheltered in the elementary school died.

Monday 4 June, Ishinomaki, Unosumai, Kesennuma

We drive back to Ishinomaki. They have constructed a new road in a series of tunnels. It is green and hilly and the farms look prosperous, ordered and surrounded by neat paddy fields and allotments on every available piece of flat land. The quality of life in the countryside looks good. I don't understand the economy here. We have been told rice consumption has been falling as people's diet becomes more Westernised. So how do they make a living?

There is snow on the distant mountains to the West. In the sunshine it

Courtyard house, Ishinomaki

is spectacularly beautiful. Large hawks soar over the fields and the hills are covered with pine trees. But there is little pasture and one sees very few farm animals. In England there would be pasture, here all hills are for timber. Every flat area is used intensively for rice and vegetables and protein comes from fish.

We are seven people in two cars. Maki is driving our car. We stop twice at service stations. The drinks are served from vending machines in cans or bottles. Coffee comes in a wide variety of flavours and seems to be ground fresh rather than instant but is hard to tell which has no sugar and I have to throw away my can because I guessed wrong. We arrive at Ishinomaki and find the office where the people from the Prefecture meet us. We file in and present our cards with lots of bowing.

The director, a smooth good-looking guy with white hair, has his photo taken with us and then disappears, leaving us with his assistants. Yuki Kawaguchi leads the presentation. Their reports look a bit like comics on cheap paper with small diagrams and photos and lots of captions and arrows. We hear about inundation heights and wave run-up and plans for new embankments. The national government's idea is to rebuild embankments and to relocate residents on higher ground to protect them against what they call a 1,000 year flood, that is a tsunami similar or a little larger than the previous event. Of course a tsunami could happen any time, but we are dealing with probability here. If there is another earthquake similar to the one in March 2011 the

Yuki Kawaguchi leads Prefecture team

Vending machines

new sea wall would be over topped again. So the plan is to move all housing in the flood zone and to raise harbours and commercial activity. Roads some distance from the shore but running parallel to it, are to be raised to 5m forming embankments that act as additional barriers behind which housing can be located. This all sounds complicated and very expensive.

We ask who has been doing the work to define flood line. Initially the young men are discomfited saying the city. But how is it that the city is able to do this complex modelling? They say that the software has been developed nationally by an earthquake Institute and applied to each settlement by consultants to come up with a recommended embankment height. We ask if people accept this. They looked confused and say that the towns' people want to have a lower height, and they have to propose other safety measures such as raising the area, evacuation centres and designated evacuation routes.

Whenever Yuki, the young man who is leading the delegation, is asked a question he says, 'that is very difficult' and consults his thick file as if he can find the answer there. I want to get on to relocation issues. I have seen a diagram in one of the reports we have been given that indicates a move from loose packed arrangements of squares to smaller rectangles in a tight grid. I ask him about it and how people feel about the higher density. He admits that in many places along the coast, where an inlet is bordered by steep tree-clad hills, they will have to carve out new terraces from the hillsides. They will try

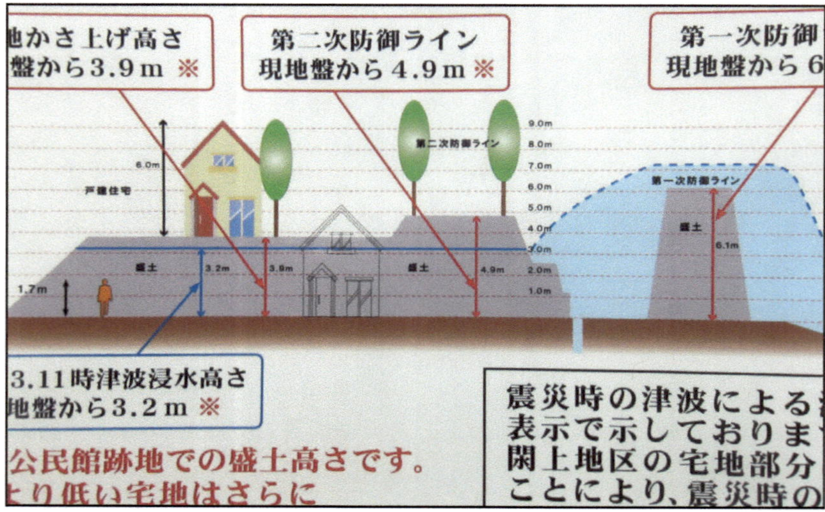

Plan for Sendai coast

to make them as close as possible to where people lived but inevitably the plots and houses will be much smaller. I ask how do people feel: they have been largely self-sufficient on their large garden plots. He says it varies and anyway it only applies to the public housing. I say that if there is less land, a shortage of builders and an increase in the cost of materials then will the cost of housing rise. They all look discomfited and say they don't know, it is not their business. It is frustrating for both sides and I realize that I am making them feel uncomfortable so I stop asking and leave questions to the others.

Finally we say our goodbyes and drive to the temporary food market they have set up in containers in the harbour. I have iced coffee and a seafood noodle dish. In the afternoon we visit a local voluntary help centre in the harbour. Two thirds of the flat land is filled with a Nippon Steel plant that came here after the war. Junichi Kano, the young man running the centre, is an architect who used to own a cake shop that was destroyed. He described how, when the warning came over the loudspeakers, he went to help people evacuate the hospital then went back home to his own house and shop in the old town near the front but was trapped by the wave and only survived because the water stopped rising leaving an 8 inch air gap below the ceiling of his bedroom. Robert rather aggressively asked him what he was doing here. I'm learning that this is his leading question because he asked the same thing in the prefecture.

Junichi Kano community worker, Kesennuma.

Junichi explains that he wanted to make a place in the town centre for the community. He didn't define its purpose. It is like a beacon in the destruction and wasteland, he says. There have been meetings to discuss the future and sessions with children to plan the new town. He said people wanted to rescue their town, that their history was important. But young people are worried that there will be no jobs. His friends, he said, had left, but said they would return. He didn't think they would. We asked would it help if the place had a high school or university. He wasn't sure there was the demand. It was interesting how he was so cheerful and positive and yet so accepting.

We drove north to the next settlement of Unosumai. Here the children of the elementary school ran when they heard the warning, but didn't wait at the first evacuation point but continued up the hill to the third and survived when the first and second evacuation points were overwhelmed. People, perhaps hundreds, sheltered in the disaster centre nearby. Even people who had reached the hills returned because it was cold. The disaster centre, despite being a huge three-storey concrete structure, was overwhelmed and everyone died. We began to get a feel for the scale of the disaster and the scale of the clean-up – lines of lorries carrying debris, massive sorting sites, and machines chopping up concrete.

We went to the next settlement and drove up the hill to the Buddhist shrine and emergency management centre. Here the sea wall and the river

Disaster management centre, Unosumai

embankment had been topped and the mayor and his 30 staff who had stayed at their posts in the municipal offices died. We can see earthworks on a nearby hill they must be clearing and terracing to relocate homes. We turn back and head back to Kesennuma where we will spend the night.

I doze but wake when we pass Rikuzentakata. There is a large flat area behind the wrecked sea defences and they are building rows and rows of 12 metre high platforms, carting all the material from the hills. It is such an orderly country that even the debris piles are regimented.

We're staying in a luxury spa in Kesennuma. It's on a hill overlooking the harbour with a pretty view of the inner bay with its tree line harbour and English-looking church. I get a shock in reception when I ask for a non-smoking room am told we were sleeping in a dormitory of five. I chose a futon nearest the door. We get taxis across town to a traditional restaurant with the usual kneeling cushions. The food was marvellous – sushi with lots of different types of fish and a tasty beef dish.

I manage to get Hitomi to help me talk to the young man from the residents' association, Miura Tomayuki. He used to teach maths in an elementary school but after the tsunami he wanted to do something for his community. I show him a matrix I have drawn with three options: the prefecture's plan to raise a high embankment along the beach, the city council plan to move the embankment back from the beach and finally the residents' plan not to have

Luxury Spa Hotel, Kesennuma

a embankment at all but to move the houses to higher ground. They plan to move the houses so one questions the reasons for a embankment. The idea of the matrix was to explain the consequences of each option clearly in relation to amenity, safety, environmental impact and cost so there could be an informed debate. He looked at the matrix a while and said how difficult it all was. Although the remaining 30 to 40-year-old young people in the community would like to explore a more radical option, older men over 70 control the residents association and the city assembly. They are very conservative, they are worried about losing central government support and are most concerned about safety. Maybe it is also about land ownership. Maybe the local people who control decision-making also own the flat land in the hazard zone and have most to lose if there is no embankment. We get a taxi back to the hotel.

Tony and I chat for a while in the lobby while the women go to the spa. We talk about the trip and what we've learnt about the economy. We talk about Turkish and Greek history. We finally get to bed after midnight. We creep in as the other three are already in bed. I spend a wakeful night dozing. Tony gets up about three. I regret forgetting to bring my earplugs but there is nothing I can do. I get up at five and shower and dress quietly.

Ballast bag temporary embankment, Oyakaigan

Tuesday 5 June, Kesennuma, Oyakaigan, Shaibatachi

It is a bright clear morning and I open the windows in the corridor and take photos of the harbour. We drive south to a beach in Oyakaigan where we meet Miura. He explains that the prefecture wants to build a 9 metre embankment that will be 40 metres wide. This was a beautiful sandy beach. He says that the beach is the basis of their identity and that they felt feel connected to the sea. The tsunami washed the sand away but it came back after a year. Most of the residents, especially the younger people, are opposed to the embankment, some feel traumatised and it is hard to get consensus.

This beach is managed by three different authorities. The Ministry of Agriculture, Forestry and Fisheries controls the northern end where the fishing boats land and the middle section, where pine wood was destroyed by the tsunami. And the southern part, where there is a road bridge over the river, is managed by the Prefectural Department of Civil Engineering.

The first they heard that they would lose the beach was in July 2012, 16 months after the disaster. Out of a population of 3,500 nearly half signed a petition to stop the plan, asking that the authorizes delay and try to find an acceptable plan. Kanaka says the central government is flexible and that the plan is only a suggestion. Miura's impression is if just one resident wants the embankment and all the rest don't, then the government will go ahead. The main problem he faces is that the community is divided. Some think it has

Looking north

been decided and there is nothing that can be done. Others have already left to make a new life elsewhere.

We climb up the black ballast bags that are piled in rows as a temporary barrier. There are broken chunks of concrete from a previous attempt to contain the ocean. The municipality want a 2.8 metre wall set back from the beach. The problem is that this will involve agreement from the Ministry of Agriculture, Forestry and Fisheries, Japan Railways, the Highways Department and the Prefecture. The deadline is June.

We go to see the temporary housing on a hill overlooking the sea. It seems way above the beach but Miura points out a red marker just down the road where the tsunami wave reached. We go on to Koesume beach. The two or three hotels and amusement park that used to be here have been washed away. An uprooted hotel still sits in the surf looking lost.

We drive back to Kesennuma and we meet Akihiko Sugawara boss of a local sake distillery. He is handsome and gently confident. All these senior figures seem to have a suave well-groomed look, wearing expensive dark suits, black shoes and tanned smiles. It seems that local businessmen in the Chamber of Commerce are opposed to the government's plans. This is a beautiful harbour with locals' boats tied up to the wharf. The tsunami reached 4–5 metres high and there is a plan for a 5 metre high embankment. Mr Sugawara says he used to live in the neighbourhood and the people never had this kind of sea defence

Hotel washed out to sea, Koesume beach Tohoku

Hotel washed out to sea, Koesume beach Tohoku

and they are opposed to a massive structure that will separate them from the sea. No one died here. They're used to living by the sea and evacuated immediately. The majority is against the plan, he says. The embankment would take up much of the flat land that is meant to protect. People believe that they can protect themselves. But while there is no agreement nothing can proceed. Meanwhile people are in temporary housing and want to start rebuilding their lives. The new deadline is October.

We drive north a few miles to Shaibatachi, a village around a beautiful small bay with large houses on terraces rising up from the narrow coastal margin. The wave was 9 metres high here and the plan is to build a wall of similar height. We have come to interview the fishermen. They are all elderly and retired from jobs in the city. They fish for sea urchin and abalone in the bay. They say the village will be ruined if the government goes ahead with the plan. 550 people lived here and only 9 died. Everyone evacuated to high ground in good time. But one person was in a wheelchair and didn't believe the wave would be so high, so elected to stay behind. The others who died went back for things they had forgotten. They think that evacuation is the best solution here plus relocation to an adjacent bluff, which is planned anyway. They say that the problem is that the head of the Prefecture is from Osaka and doesn't understand the situation here.

Akhiko Sugawara, owner of saki distillery

Height of proposed embankment, Shaibatachi

In town we meet with a Professor of Urban Planning at Kogakuin University who has good English and explains the dilemmas the city faces, including dealing with the huge boat that was washed inland. I would like to speak to him more but Hitomi whisks us away to the City Council offices to meet Takeshi Ogata and his wife.

Stranded boat, Kesennuma

Mr Ogata is an assembly member and his family is one of the most established in the area. The Ogata house was built in 1810 and has been in the family ever since. They had just had it re-thatched it eighteen months earlier at a cost of £70,000. His wife described how her grandmother had told her to close the shutters when a tsunami was coming. She had closed them and was trying to start the car but had changed her mind and had run up the hill behind the house. The house was washed away by the wave. Mr Ogata showed as photographs of a beautiful low-rise long-house with a deep thatched roof. They had a photo after the tsunami of the roof of the house washed up on the beach like an upturned boat. They have recovered a third of the roof timbers and a university plans to reconstruct the house if they can raise the money. Ogata was most pressing in giving as photographs of his lost home. I asked him about the plans for the town. He said that there was no consensus in the assembly but that it doesn't make sense to build such high embankments when they are relocating everyone.

Ogata House, Kesennuma, before and after tsunami

We gather at the temporary market in town and Miura buys us croquettes. I have a quick chat to Robert and Prof Kurata but Emily herds us off; we have to drive back to Sendai and it is late. We drive through Matushima, a holiday resort where line of offshore islands broke the power of the wave. We found out later this was influential in thinking in Iwanuma where we are going tomorrow. We drive through a small hamlet were people sheltered in the elementary school and died. We stop at a 7-11 and I buy food since we'll get back late.

Wednesday 6 June, Iwanuma

Today we have interviews with the authorities in Iwanuma to hear about plans for the Millennium Hope Hills. The vice-mayor describes that as well as building a 7 metre embankment and moving people to a new raised settlement, they plan to create a park with a line of fifteen 10 m high hills linked by a causeway. As well as providing a refuge they also think the hills will reduce the power of the wave like the islands off Matushima. It will cost ¥4 billion and the government has promised to pay half. We drive to the site and the mayor, grey-haired and smiling, gives a polished speech that Maki nobly translates. He says the hills will be an educational facility where people can come, reflect, learn and pray. Made from debris, they are literally built on people's lives. The embankment will not last forever, but the hills will go on giving protection, he says. There is a dedication ceremony this Sunday and people will come and plant trees. I ask Maki to help me translate the species list we have been given

Vice-Mayor of Natori

Millenium Hope Hills

using her portable digital dictionary. It works and I recognise lots of plants that Scharlie uses in her gardens. We drive to see the new settlement and how they are raising the level of the land. We drive to Natori City to meet city planners Aizawa Yukiya and Sako Hitoshi. They explain that unlike places further north, this area is growing because of its good transport links with an international airport and bullet train. They tell us about plans for Yuriagi that we visited on our first day. The wave was over 9m high; there were 958 deaths and 4,500 people are still living in temporary housing.

They plan multiple lines of defence: the embankment, a raised road, and the main highway. They have mapped two hazard zones, one for industry and one near the river where they will raise the land and resettle people. But the scheme is controversial. In July last year a third of people said they were prepared to return to the proposed site. By April the proportion dropped to a quarter.

Yuriagi has a long history as a fishing port with a nice beach. They hope people will return and the place will recover its charm. I ask if so many people are fearful of coming back have they a Plan B. They say that they are investigating a site to the west of the national road but they are worried that there won't be enough people to justify the expense of the engineering works. I suggest that since the area is growing maybe new people will want to move here. The new public housing will be 5 to 6 stories and will provide

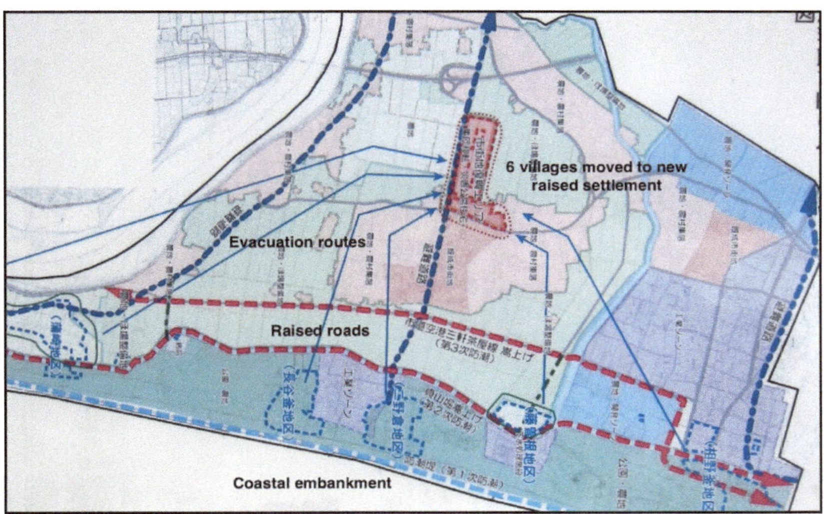

Plan for Iwanuma: embankment, raised roads, new raised village and escape routes

an evacuation point. There is also a loan subsidy for those wanting to build their own homes outside Yuriagi. Previously each family had their own plot. In the new scheme these will be much smaller or non-existent. The planners say there are resident groups who prefer to move inland.

We drive back into Sendai to visit a new research institute of disaster science at Tohoku University. Professors Masato Matusaki and Fumahiko Iwamura are the leading lights. Prof Iwamura describes how decision-making in Japan is monolithic and that is very difficult to propose a different process to the national government. The area is in decline, so he is not optimistic. The elderly want to go back to how it was before, he says, but there isn't the new energy and ideas to get things moving. Yuichi Ono says he lived abroad for 20 years and since he returned has been surprised that decision-making is less top-down than he expected. David Alexander says the central government wants harmonisation and accountability while the local area needs choice and tailored-made solutions and that this is a dilemma. Kanaka says that history can be a source of information to help people make good decisions and that this influences the move to higher ground. I say hello to Prof Iwamura and give him Robin's greetings and say his welcome in Cambridge. Anawat, who organised our trip earlier in the week, is very impressive. Although he is young and he looks as though he is a high flyer.

Then back to the hotel to grab my Japan Railcard and off to the station

Yuriaga, Sendia

to drop off the hire car and get tickets for tomorrow's journey to Kobe and Kyoto. Unfortunately, I bring the Railcard voucher and not the actual card. Maki and I have to walk back to the hotel and get it. Fortunately it's not far and the process is quite painless. There is a young musician singing pop songs outside the station. He is not very good and straining his voice but a young woman is dancing and encouraging her toddler to join in.

We grab a taxi to the restaurant to meet the others. I order beef tongue curry with salad. It is fantastic and the salad is fresh. We are all in good form. This has been a great trip, well organised and without any stress or agro, at least in part to Tony's low-key approach. He is gentle and well-prepared. We go on by taxi to a bar in the red light district and Emily orders for me. We're kneeling again which I find impossible. So I get a pile of cushions and lean against the wall. Anton tells stories about kidnapping brides in Bulgaria and Jack says that tradition still persists in China but in a playful way between the couple's friends. Anton says the best thing to do when you have to get up early to catch a plane is to stay up all night. He has been visiting a bar near the hotel and getting three hours sleep a night. He says he missed his plane because he overslept and the next time to avoid the same mistake he went to the airport early and, having a couple of hours to wait, fell asleep at the gate and missed his flight again. Trying to get money out of an ATM machine he thought the instructions said to enter his passport. But the machine gobbled it up and he had to call an engineer to get it back. He seems a little accident-prone for a nuclear engineer. We get a taxi back to the hotel and Anton goes off to his bar and I go off to bed.

Last night, beef tongue restaurant, Sendai

Thursday 7 June, Kobe

I meet Maki in the lobby at 7.30 sharp and we walk to the station. We are in plenty of time. Trains in Japan stop exactly, so people know exactly where to queue for their carriage. But we're waiting at the wrong end of the platform and have to battle our way to the car at the front of the train. We pass Mount Fuji that there is low cloud I get only a glimpse. But it is bigger than I expected and I can see snow.

We buy a Bento and share it. It is luxurious; fresh fish rice and pickled vegetables. I love the food here. We change trains in Tokyo. We arrive and climb the stairs to ground level. Suddenly it is hot and sunny. Summer has arrived in Kobe. I have run out of money and we try a couple of ATMs without success. I check my guide book that says that they accept foreign cards in post offices or City Bank. We try both but my bank refused the transaction. I have some dollars and Euros I can change. I can't ring my bank because my phone has run out of battery.

We give up and get a taxi to the International Recovery Platform offices. We get there half an hour late and I plug in my phone to charge it. There are five people on their side. I say who I am and they give me an overview of the IRP. We get on to the Great East Japan Earthquake and I pitch in with my idea about consultation based on options. Perhaps because they see the bigger picture they are unwilling to except anything is wrong with the current approach. Sanjaya insists responsibility has been delegated to the local authorities and Shingo, a clever Japanese recovery expert, says that round table discussion and a slow considered approach to decision-making has been

Shinkansen 'bullet train' to Kobe

the basis of Japanese society since a typhoon in 1961.

Nevertheless I persist and provide examples from Kesennuma and Yuriagi of where the system seems to be failing. I apologise for implying any criticism and insist that I'm only suggesting a greater preparedness in planning consultation in advance and developing a method of options so they can be an informed debate. They get the idea that they remain urbane and imply they already do all this. I'm not convinced. I show them the CAR website and recovery documents and they save the link to their site.

My phone is charged so I ring my bank from the taxi and discover I've been trying to withdraw £275 and my daily limit is £250. We catch a local stopping train and in Kyoto Maki takes me to the post office and then finds my hotel. The station in Kyoto is huge and daunting and the hotel is a forbidding brick box. But it's deceptive. I change my room to a non-smoking. It's a double and at a bit more expensive but I'll appreciate the extra room. I explain to Maki that my father was a heavy smoker and now I can't bear the smell of cigarette smoke. She asked if he died of cancer and I say yes and she seems very moved. I discover later that her mother is dying of lung cancer.

The room is great and I feed the long cable from the Internet under the bed out of the way, sit at my computer on the desk and do the usual catching up. Maki is busy tonight so I have asked another student from Kyoto who came on the trip. Farnaz Mahdavian is Iranian and has been living in Kyoto for three years. She would like to study for her Ph.D. in the States or the UK. We meet in the lobby at 7.30. I have found a place called Taku Taku that sounds interesting and has food and live music. Farnaz plugs the address into her iPhone and we set off, first back to the station to take the subway a couple of stops and then, with help from a couple of strangers, we find the place hidden in a courtyard behind the houses. Farnaz says so many of the special things about Japan are hidden or secret.

There is a loud pop music coming from the building and I'm not sure I made the right choice. II wonder if I'll be able to hear myself think. It is quite expensive but you get one free drink. We take off our shoes and climb the stage at the back and find a couple of stools to perch on. The band is four guitars, drummer and lead singer. He has long hair wild eyes and a very theatrical performance. His voice is okay but the songs not that great. Halfway through the set the drummer changes. A girl with long black hair pushes her way onto the stage, takes the sticks and the music takes off. She's really great. I don't know why they don't ditch the boy and let her play all the time. Farnaz is enjoying it and it turns out to have been a good idea after all.

We find a table once the music stops and order curry, noodles and more beer. She tells me about her family in Iran. Her father is an earthquake engineer working on dams. She has an older sister and a 21-year-old brother who is Down's syndrome. Her mother gave her up her job as a teacher to look after him. She shows me a photo of the beautiful marquetry he does. He goes to work at a centre and gets a small salary and wants to have an exhibition of his work. She plans to go back to Iran one day but not yet while things are so bad for women. She says she can stay in Japan. She has lots of colleagues but has only made one or two friends. Japanese boys are very difficult, she says, and don't seem to want to grow up. Farnaz takes me back to the station and points me in the right direction for the hotel, which is just as well since I'm tipsy and would probably have got lost.

Friday 8 June, Kyoto

I get up early and go to the station to find breakfast. I manage to buy biscuits to take home for the office, buy a day pass for the bus and find a nice cafe for a scrambled egg roll and coffee. Despite loving the fresh fish, pickles and spicy sweetmeats, I can't quite face rice or noodles for breakfast. Back at the hotel

Shop, Silver Pavilion Temple Road

I manage to check-in the flight to Hong Kong. I get started after 10 and find the bus stop near the station. There is quite a queue but I get on okay. There is heavy traffic so I don't reach the temple till 12.

On the way to the temple there is a beautiful shop. On an impulse I go in and look for a present for Scharlie. I hate knick-knacks but I can't resist and buy a wooden bowl and a lacquer ware jug in black and Japanese red. I've come to the Silver Temple because my guide says it's nicer than the more famous Golden Temple and the garden is beautiful. The road steepens and is lined with gift shops and ice cream parlours. The temple does not disappoint. I like the sand gardens that are designed to reflect moonlight. I climb up to the lookout and take pictures. I haven't decided what to do next. The guide book mentions a mountain behind the temple called Diamond Peak. It says it takes two hours. I only have my shiny shoes, having forgotten to bring my trainers. I decide to have a look and find myself following 30 boys in climbing boots. The path climbs steeply. It is hot, but the way is shaded by trees. An old man seems to be trying to keep pace with me on the long line of steps that leads to the shrine. I stride out on the narrow kerb and leave him far behind. How childish! But how great to feel strong pain free and enjoy walking again.

At the shrine I sit on the steps, take off my shoes and enjoy the view. The old boy arrives, smiles and nods and also takes off his boots. The view is good.

Pagoda, Ginkaku-ji Silver Temple. Kyoto

Sand sculpture Silver Temple

Top of Diamond Peak, Kyoto

It is a bright sunny day and I can see Kyoto University and the Imperial Palace. After a rest I decide to go on. There is a steep set of steps and I don't know how far it is to the summit. There are lots of people descending so I have to push my way up and step aside to let people pass. It is much further than I thought. The track winds steeply up through the forest. I am tired and my legs

Rickshaw, Silver Pavilion Temple Road

Philosophers' Path Kyoto

protest. Finally I reached the top. There is a concrete trig point and bamboo benches and I find the spot. I drink some more of my water, glad I filled my bottle in the spring of the start of the climb.

Lots of little girls about three or four years old arrive. I'm most impressed they got up here. They line up in front of me looking over the drop to the city and all shout trying to get an echo. Then three little girls find small stones and start throwing them. One trips on the edge but steadies herself and jinks around. No one seems bothered. They have a teacher with them and teenage helpers. It's all very relaxed. I sit nodding off in the sunshine. It's pleasant and I'm glad I came.

Finally, it's time to go and I head off down. It's more difficult in my Chelsea boots than coming up. But with the help of a rope handrail I manage the steep bits. It's amazing but one is always surprised by how far one has climbed. I

Temple Philosophers' path.

Private house Philosophers' path.

find the ice cream shop and order a mixed green tea and vanilla ice cream cone. I am hot and tired and sitting in the cream parlour licking the cone is marvellously restorative. At the end of the hill of shops there is a canal running across the slope of the mountains and a stone path by its side known as the philosopher's path. It is shady under the cherry trees and the water is limpid clear and rushing quickly over the green weed. A narrow road runs parallel to the canal serving beautiful houses. Some have large gardens. This looks a wealthy area. The city is obviously full of hidden gems. I am tired and my feet hurt so I stop on convenient benches of stone. At a shrine I wash my hands and rinse my mouth before offering my gift of small change and ringing the bell to waken the God. I go on. The path ends but I continue along the road to a large monastery. Finally I head downhill and find the bus stop. I run for the bus and drift off to sleep in the dense traffic back to Kyoto station.

Rather than go back to the hotel straightaway I decide to explore. The station is vast. There are nine floors of high-class shops above ground. I go up the escalators to a deck running north-south at the end of the building. Looking back the roof is spectacular. It is a steel lattice work not unlike the ironwork of a Victorian station, open at either end, creating a vast cathedral like space. The escalators end in a flight of steps like an amphitheatre and lots of people are sitting as if waiting for a concert. In fact the whole space is thronging with people dressed in bright colours, ascending and descending and circulating between the balcony cafes and restaurants perched over the void. The whole thing is enchanting and I'm glad I made the effort. I cross to the opposite side were the escalators go all the way to the roof and is a set of steps to a garden shrine on the roof. I sit a minute.

This is a huge emporium and the third and second floors are restaurants and cafes. I find a cake shop and buy a coconut cake and a mouthwatering pear in wrapped in filo pastry to take back to the hotel. I change into a kimono and make green tea. There is time for a quick half hours sleep. I set the alarm and fall into a deep slumber. I wake refreshed shower and shave and I'm nearly ready when Maki rings to say they are in the lobby.

Kyoto railway station

I meet Prof Kiyono. He's about my height and has a warm smile and a firm handshake. I like him immediately. We set off walking. He says we're going to a bar about 15 minutes walk. It's called Kura Kura. There are booths were clients take off their shoes. We sit at the bar. They seem to know him here and the places are reserved for us. The food is fabulous – sushi, oyster and beef. We drink beer. I lose count. The talk flows. My impressions of Japan; his reflections on Japanese character. He says their worldview is too narrow and that they need to change. Sending his students abroad is part of this. One of his best student is here tonight with Maki and he has brought the paperwork for me to sign for her internship at CAR. I read it carefully despite the alcohol and sign. I praise Maki for her organisation and hard work and say how exceptional I thought the trip went.

We talk about Kiyono's time in England and about rugby he played for his school. The first time he went to England they toured around playing different schools and always losing. He described how a team from Oxford arrived half an hour late and Kiyono asked why and was told gentleman could afford to be late. I was incensed and said they were no gentleman. I felt ashamed. Kiyono said the food in Cambridge was very expensive. His favourite pub was the Eagle. He was impressed when I told him what I'd done that day and about the live music last night. He asked how I knew about such things. I said I'd read about them or they had been recommended. I'm invited to a barbecue tomorrow. From here we catch a taxi to another bar tucked behind a house at the end of a narrow passage. There is no sign on the one would know it was here. It's called Shiraki and run by a delightful woman with short cropped hair and a big personality he calls Mama Sen Miko. She's friendly. She lives alone with her Jack Russell. She asked if I'd had a pet and I tell her about our cat Chelo. We talk about death and what will want done with our bodies. Maki says she wants to be scattered to the winds and come back as an animal or a plant or a rock. Or a piece of plastic says Kiyono. I'm pretty sozzled by now, drinking potato alcohol on the rocks. It slips down painlessly. We walked to the main road, me trying to keep straight on the white line painted to mark the pedestrian sidewalk. We say good night and they bundle me into a taxi. Kiyono says it's paid for and it will take me back to my hotel.

Saturday 9 June, Kyoto, Tokyo

I breakfast in the hotel, at a pleasant table near the window watching people walk by. We catch a taxi. It seemed quite close to Kawai Kanjiro's house on the map but it takes a long while. We arrive five minutes early. Other Japanese couples arrive. They open exactly at 10 o'clock. Everything here is so well ordered.

We enter the house and take off our shoes in the hallway and put on slippers. I leave my jacket in a lockbox. The house is timber frame with dark polished wood floors and in a criss-cross pattern that is Korean. Japan invaded Korea in the 30s and Kawai was highly influenced by Korean folk art and ordinary everyday objects and patterns. I notice a wooden grille in the floor and Maki finds out it was an air raid shelter during the war. I'm really impressed with the simple elegance of the house. It feels very modern yet in the style of a traditional Japanese home. It seems Kawai designed it himself in 1937 when he moved here to set up his pottery.

We explore the ground floor first, the simple gravel courtyard with its green plants, no colour and boardwalk paths. The roof overhangs so the windows are simple sliding screens; glass on the outside and paper on the inner leaf. There is a photo of Kawai at work, concentrating. There is a well with a pulley, a small

Kawai Kanjiro house

Hallway entrance

Kawai Kanjiro house

Beckoning cat

room for the tea ceremony and a clay oven for baking. There are a number of Windsor style chairs that were apparently from Bernard Leach, an English potter with whom Kawai worked. At the rear of the courtyard, where the site rises, is a massive updraught kiln. It is arranged as a series of brick rooms with a thick clay roof. The fire is lit at the bottom of the slope and the differential heat in each succeeding space gives different firing temperatures and different glazes. Apparently Kawai worked with other potters and they fired their work together. We see where he worked at a low wheel sunk into the floor so he could sit at floor level with his feet in a pit surrounding the wheel.

Maki points out the stone beckoning cat a traditional symbol in Japan.

Potter's wheel

Kawai Kanjiro

Upstairs the bedrooms are spacious and light and floured with tatami. All is elegant and well tempered with views into the courtyard.The staircase is quite small with boxlike drawers either side and a rope threaded with wooden beads to aid your descent. To get furniture up there is a convenient rope and pulley in the two height space in the centre of the house which brings light into the inner space of the ground floor and allows heat from the open pit fire to circulate. I sit at Kawai's desk in his study. I'm intrigued by the details: the convenient storage, the occasional carving, the finely wrought iron hooks.

Pulley over two height space

Kanjiro's desk

River, Kyoto

Syomen Dori bridge, Kyoto

Finally it is time to leave. I had been hoping to see a little of the old town and get my chance to see more of Japanese domestic architecture. There are new houses in a traditional style. It is a road of geishas and we see one or two posing for pictures. I'm not I am not sure what it is all about and asked Maki if they are still concubines. She says they used to be but now their role is only theatrical. We cross a bridge over a wide river. Some men are fishing. In summer Maki says the terraces that line the banks are restaurants.

We take a train and reach the pebble beach on a river were the barbecue is happening. There are hundreds picnicking and at first Maki can't find our group. I regret bringing my jacket. I didn't know if it was going to be posh. Everyone is welcoming and Prof Kyoto introduces me to his colleagues. I drink green tea because I still feel hung over after yesterday. I have some meat, salmon and

Kiyono's Laboratory bar-b-que

vegetables. Prof Kiyono and I end up chatting convivially on stools under an umbrella. He suggests that I should go to the shrine nearby and that Farnaz should take me and see me back to my hotel so she can to chat about her future. I give Maki a big hug. I've grown very fond of her. I shake Prof Kiyono's hand warmly.

There are three shallow bottomed boats at the entrance to the shrine. There didn't seem to be enough water in the river to float them so I'm intrigued. They are bigger than Cambridge punts with a curved bottom and raised stern and prow.

We catch a train to Farnaz's favourite place, a river where she comes on her 50 cc motorbike to sit at night. There is a weir and boats similar to ones we saw in the shrine. They punted from the front Oxford style. There is a small railway upstream that crosses the mountain to the next province and

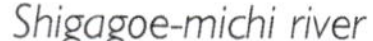

Shigagoe-michi river

the boats links it by a one hour river journey.

We take the train back to Kyoto station and find a cafe in the main atrium space to have ice coffee and cheesecake. Farnaz tells me her plans and asked if she should try for study in Britain or the States. I say she would like living in London if she could afford it. I deeply regret the careless way I said her proposed topic was not strong enough last week. But she is determined and Prof Kiyono encouraged her and told me he thinks she will make it. So I'll introduce her to people and see if I can help. We talk about her life in Japan how good it is been but lonely. I tell her about my time in Venezuela. I want to tell her that life gets easier but I know I've been very lucky. She will need luck and a bit of help. I collect my bags in the hotel left luggage and we sit on the sofa while I sort myself out to make sure I have my tickets and passport. Farnaz takes me to the station. We say goodbye and I turn and wave and see her looking forlorn.

Kyoto train station

Farnaz

The bullet train is fantastic and the changeover to the Narita express easier than I imagined. But I'm exhausted and have a blisters on my heel from my inappropriate shoes. It serves me right for travelling light. The hotel is marvellous and such good value at £35 a night. It's really luxurious. On an impulse I go in the first restaurant I come to and order tuna, rice and pickles with miso soup followed by green tea ice cream.

I have a bath, which is unusual for me. Then it set the alarm. The rest of the journey is long but relaxing. I'm becoming a seasoned traveller without realising it – much more relaxed than I used to be much and less fearful. I write a list of all my pending jobs on the leg to Hong Kong. I miss my train by a couple of minutes and have cheesecake on the balcony in King's Cross. Home after another big trip.

りんくうタウン
宅展示場

www.ingramcontent.com/pod-product-compliance
Lightning Source LLC
LaVergne TN
LVHW052300100826
845147LV00001B/102

* 9 7 8 1 9 1 2 4 6 0 0 4 5 *